ART OF
DISILLUSIONMENT

David Synn

Editor: Eva Xanthopoulos
theartisticmuse.com/poehemian-press.html

Cover Art & Illustrations: JC Bravo
www.jcbravo.com

Author Photo: David Stephenson
www.davidtstephenson.com

Author Website: www.davidsynn.com

This book is dedicated to my brother, Danny.

12/12/1979 - 4/18/2009

TABLE OF CONTENTS

ACKNOWLEDGMENTS

I would like to thank my wife and best friend Missy Kondakdjian for all her love and support, my parents for raising me to be the person I am today, David Stephenson and JC Bravo for the amazing photography and artwork that went into this book, and all my friends and family for believing in me.

No matter how dark things seem, you are never alone. If you ever feel that you just can't take life, suicide is never the solution. There is hope and there is help. www.suicidepreventionlifeline.org

The Vision

Interpretation gets lost in translation.
Speaking in tongue, ambiguously
avoiding the question. Deceiver
of the times—no different than those
who came before him.

Once asked about his vision, he
replied that he only had the purest
of intentions. An instrument of death,
leading the lamb to the slaughterhouse;
The piper.

Demigod—his smile on every
television set. The vision
of the community blurred into a frenzy.
Rock star—his song no different
than those who came before him.

Peeping Tom

The Voyeur
lives vicariously
through the lives of others—
Unseen by the untrained eye.

Information age.
He scrolls through his victims.
The predator—The prey.
Masked by integrity.
Espionage.

With a jaded heart, he searches
for something while looking
to others for the thing he does not.

A Slave to My Addiction

Premeditated act,
Self-mutilation,
Addiction runs deeper than the user.
A drinker—self-induced vomiting
not about weight. *Discipline.*

My problems go down the drain.
The junkie, lying to himself to keep
the frame. Can't hear "you look sick"
enough times. Can never be too thin.

Killing myself slowly. The mirror shows
a man whose waning world is crumbling
to the foundation brick-by-brick. In control
while on my knees. *Poetry.*

Need to feed. Incomplete. Cycle never
ends. Feeling wrists to see improvement,
spitting blood, and nosebleeds. Hiding any
trace of binging. *Control fading.*

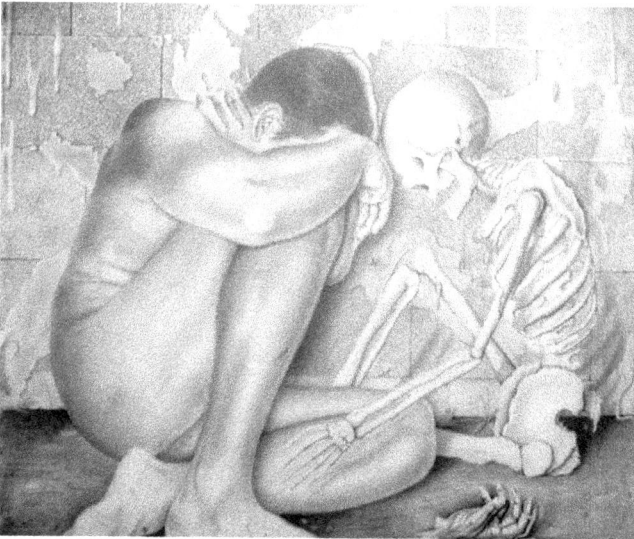

Gods of Deceit

The knife severs the heart—
Separating, disconnecting
to the disbelief of the naïve.

Keep the friend closer
than your enemy. The Devil.
One evil seen. Gods of deceit.

From the wound, dragged into
the desert heat. Ripped open.
Cackling hyenas ready to feed.

Breaking Silence

The silence, deafening
like a siren. Blinding lights
meant for distraction, it's
just a matter of timing.

When to scream, to bleed
or when to break something.
Massaging the crevices
of the walls bruises
my fingertips.

Family photos in cheap frames,
knick-knacks, incense
and an Elvis Presley piggy bank.
She said he was for a rainy day.

I've resorted to counting
the splinters in the sub-flooring.
Trash that needs to be thrown
away. The TV on mute, flashing.

The nothingness, emptiness has
companioned me for a decade.
Screaming in vain. Deafened
by the rage that defines me.

Contradiction in the Color Gray

Filled with questions
about my own morality.
Conviction, hunger,
and starvation. Pornography
or salvation. Damnation.
Honor and the color gray.
Everything finds a way
to the top only to be
brought back down
to the start. The motions.

I retire to the corner,
Sitting and staring
intently at the wall—
A black hole.
Gazing at the sun.
Either or, inconsistent
with itself before it begins.
I am at war with the notion
that chivalry is dying.
Indifference.

I'll see it through
to the end. No answers
given. No questions really
asked. I sit in my corner
reflecting on the past,
the future, the present.
Stumbling along, blinded
with no assistance, I
only see the color gray—
Walking contradiction.

Ghost

Brushed to the side
by the crowd.
Smoking cigarette,
Security blanket. *Inadequate.*

The ghost, neither a liquid
nor a solid. Phasing his way
into the bar scene. *Insecurity.*

Center of the universe. Failed
perception. Crippled with anxiety,
he leaves. *Absence unnoticed.*

Damaged

The playback in my head
constantly on repeat.
Distortion.

Blood pours down my
face. Only the whites
of my hazel eyes show.

Impressions of the scars
remind me of all the times
I should have left that hell.

Head held together
with bare hands for days
to avoid getting stitches.

Coward
Enabler
Monster

Magnificent Liars

Who are you trying to fool?
Who are you trying to use?
A wolf in sheep's blood
covered from head to shoe,
reeking of hypocrisy.

Manipulative, left to my own
devices. Two sides to every
coin. Two faces—one shown.
The other cloaked
in the subconscious.

We don't tell the truth
to soften a blow or to get out
of doing time for our crimes.
Magnificent in our grandeur,
we lie—it's our nature.

Season of the Vagabond

Sundown. Punch in. Lights out.
Fenced in with the addicts
and schizophrenics...

The routine.

Rules don't apply. No one abides,
Domestic violence. Noncompliance,
Statutory rape and barbed wire gates.

The unknown soldier, Post Traumatic
Stress Disorder. Shell-shocked, he hits
the floor. *The war I don't remember.*

Punch out. Trekking
into the elements. Systematic
in nature. Back in time for the sunset.

The Great Illusion

Delusions and parallels
tied together by strings
of fabricated parables.
Standing at The Alpha,
The Omega. Wandering
a barren existence.

Can't decide if I'm
inside or on the outside.
The Icon, The Phenom.
Pay no attention
to the man behind the curtain—
The great illusion.

Rise of the contender,
Undisputed title defender,
The watcher of mankind.
Cross I bare. The lie.
Shattering into hundreds
of fragmented pieces.

Perpetual State of Insomnia

Fluttering images flash
behind the lids of my eyes,
Subconscious divides
as the body plays tricks on my
mind. Awake in my slumber,

I dreamt about snakes. My legs
once again could not carry my
weight. The recurring dream,
Walking the streets at night.
Bruised from falling—Deception.

Pulling back the covers. Sweating
uncontrollably, I count sheep to
get my mind to rest. Back on my
feet. The day job. Drinking large
quantities of coffee to function.

The sugar never helps. I keep
walking the streets. Feet buckling
underneath me, melting into the
concrete. Constantly awake in a
manifested dream state.

Reflections of Disenchantment

Michelangelo or Van Gogh?
My masterpiece goes
the way of the martyrs. Legacy
as dead as my heroes.
Future is history.

Turning to dust, no rising
from the ashes. No fiery phoenix.
The spoken poet, the stand up comic,
the musician peddling on the streets
to survive. The astonishment.

Mourning the fallen. I look to my
predecessors for some sort
of condolence. They don't talk anymore.
I've hit rock bottom too many times
to pick myself off the floor.

Prostitute

Disease underneath the fingernails—
The epidemic, the whore fought
her way through the streets to be
used. It's all she's known. Could
be worse—She puts her shoes on.

Cocaine abuse, mascara running.
The combination puts stress on
her now rough-looking exterior.
Property of a man from time to time,
spitting out blood from his punches.

Sleeps on an air mattress when
she's not in bed with pigs. *Filth.*
Can't wash it away, prays to a god
that she doesn't know exists the next time
she takes her pills, she succeeds.

Suppression of a Memory

Rhythm off time again,
Never was too good
at keeping time. Don't even
know what time it really is,
Out of sync with the beat.

Lost my sense of direction,
Chasing after a memory
as incomplete as the man racing
against the clock to retrieve—
Conditioning is the key.

Head hurts from last night's
beating. Don't remember
the scenery or reason, don't know
what I'm chasing after anymore.
Moving backwards in motion.

There's a connection between
a murderer and the gun that
I am holding. Too confused
to put it together until the end.
The beginning.

The Music Is Over

Wasting away.
A beautiful scene in ruins,
Sucked clean to the marrow,
Stuck in reality. I had talent,
appreciated for its overall
unpredictability.

Creative highs, critical praise.
The price I paid to be brought
down so low beneath the earth.
None of us get out alive. Men
in their 40s barely breathing—
Do not resuscitate.

The legacy, washed-up.
Has-been. Never-was.
Living the dream, living to die.
In Charleston West Virginia,
no hope or future in front of us,
The music is over.

Burning City

Sketchy looking things going
down on the east end of town.
They're bringing in the drugs
from the bordering west.
Smoking gun in hand,
the policeman stands above
the body of someone's
beloved pet. Bulletproof vest.

Kings, queens and juvenile
teens spend all their time
cooking methamphetamines.
Veins shot from hypodermics.
No time to rest, baby needs
to be fed. The welfare
of the community is measured
by the digits on a check.

No need to feed on this disease,
The city is burning, fighting
to take back the rights we never had.
Illusion of freedom.

Loosing sight is easy when justice
is blind. Sitting here safely
behind my keyboard, waiting for
the day they kick down my door.

Motel

Stripped myself of identity—dignity.
Hands shaking. The mask, flaking.
The smile, painted on. The universe
revolves around my own state
of disillusionment. Settle into my room.

Laying on the bed, nauseous
from vertigo. Room spinning in circles,
Candle in the Wind is on the radio,
Drinking with the king tonight,
Sublime as I dim the lights.

Sometimes I wonder, who was here
before. Most of the time, it doesn't
bother me at all. Only here awhile.
Someone could have been burned
alive. The yellowing of the paint.

The stain on the ceiling—The stink.
Sometimes I wish God would wash
me away with the rats. The foam
and the disease. I see one now looking back
at me. Savage little creature of the night.

Soul Mates

Porcelain rubs against
the ink in my skin,
Cracking and chipping
away in the end?
Pushing apart until one
of us starts to bleed.

I am a carving a stone
made of dust and alone,
Blown away with the
ashes of the unknown,
Turning to clay for the
remainder of my days.

Not a mystery to you,
seeing through my rust.
Although we thought
forever, your love eluded
me. Blood pours
from my porcelain cup.

Estranged. As time slowed,
we both grew older
and apart—Wasn't supposed to
be this way. Withering
away into our hollow hell,
Spiraling into nothingness.

Through you I've learned
to separate. Sensations feel
real and intimate to the touch.
Though not to be,
we will forever remain
soul mates.

Fear

What we need is
more fear to feed,
More hate to spread rapid
like a viral disease.
Constantly self-destructing,
Mother Earth is bleeding,
She needs an abortion.

Fear is what we read,
What we bleed and breathe,
It's what's on the radio
and the television screen—
People should not be afraid,
It's only man-made laws
they intend to take.

Given a face every few years,
Mass hysteria pursues, meaning
never truly evident or clear.
What we need is more pop stars
and teen magazines,
Something to get our minds
off the issues at hand.

The bible.

So many relate. It's fear
keeping them from crossing
the line of what is real
and what is divine,
Picking and choosing the
parts they want to believe.
So do we as a society.

Death.

Ignorant in our elation,
Never knowing the hour
of what is inevitable.
Like the story so old,
If a rotting tree falls,
and no one hears it,
does it make a sound?

Of course.

By not knowing, you forfeit
all and any sense of caring.
Enter current surroundings,
you search for some direction.
We are all linked by it, whether
you fear the law of your land
or the creator that made it.

People should not be afraid,
It's only a matter of time
before you won't care at all.
Make the best of your days,
Be kind to your brother
and to your mother, for she
is the one who is bleeding.

Man on the Ledge

Examining the bricks, I run my
hand over cement covered
in graffiti and spit. Someone was
here before. Saliva is dry—cold.
Did they jump? Climb back
in the window? Maybe a Good Samaritan
talked them down, crashed
into the ground,
Bones shattering.

Legs buckling underneath
my body, I look over the 40-story
drop. What's keeping me from
taking that step? Looking
down, so high above the earth.
The sky, a reddish purple.
A bat-winged gargoyle ready
to take flight. A superhero.

I want to savor this moment.
Breathe in the fresh air
from the city that abandoned me.
Nauseous as I look down into the void.
The phone is ringing, I hear it ring
for what seems like hours through
the open window sill. Whoever it is,
it better be worth answering.

Social Disease

Return to the apes. No more
a black or white fight then Christian
to Muslim. Propaganda spinning,
No one's listening, no one's thinking,
A picture worth a thousand words,
Meaningless distractions.

The odd duck singled out regardless
of ethnicity. Human nature. The heart bleeds
red from the wounds of the population,
Black man on the news again. Terrorists.
Soccer mom lets her kid run rampant,
Model citizen with a Xanax addiction.

Majority decision rules while our children
learn less and less about history. It repeats.
Pawns, puppets and con artists. Painting
the picture that everything is fine through
social networking and rigged elections.
The art of human extinction.

The Actor, The Singer, The Fighter, The Mongrel

I am the actor.
All this shame,
I bow in forever after.
Hide my face behind the eyes
of a stranger, was born
to play this role. They said I'd
go far as I spiral further
and further out of control.

I am the singer.
I recreated the art of the genre,
Blew my vocal chords hitting
the note heard around the world—
They always favored the scream,
Hit it hard in the desert heat,
Blisters tattoo my throat.

I am the fighter.
The heavy-weight champion
of mediocrity.
Posing for pictures as my
face is torn piece by piece.
I hate my life, I hate my wife.
Last strand of dignity,
The ring forever calling.

I am the mongrel.
Alone and pitiful,
Voices laughing
in my general direction,
Panic ensues and fuels my
frustration. Commitments
to fulfill. Screaming silently,
Praying for death to find me.

The Fool

The fool who knows nothing
of remorse, knows all he needs
to know. Ignorant in his apathetic
retort, he finds no peace
in the sins he repeats. Blissful,
he searches for pleasures for his
self-indulgence.

I'm a fool. It was you I turned
to when times were hard. Took
advantage, my delicate dove.
A free man, though in chains,
Imprisoned and held captive
at my own transgression.
Misery infinite.

You, the angel, set free with
clipped wings and severed soul.
Back from whence you came—
The unknown. The fool who
knows it all knows nothing
except that he is lonely
and heartbroken.

Pop Culture

As I sit, I ponder the vast
world of pop culture. To
myself, I wonder how
to keep up with every
form and sub-genre.

It's all about how much—
How much you know and how
far you'll go to keep up
with the times on a playing
field that continually grows.

When is it too old to use slang
meant for a sixteen year old?
Knowing your fifteen won't happen?
Fooled by Warhol, an ape could
have made a better prediction.

Consumerism paves the way
to shopping sprees in streets
of gold. The American Dream—
Fabricated from wars
and conspiracy. Fashion
and run ways.

The 1990s.

What's on the TV? Commercials
meant to spark your interest
and shows filled with a false
sense of reality. People can't
seem to see through it.

We are blinded by machines
and the want to fit into society.
As one trend dies, it is replaced by

another, from a darker past and world.
Over and over again, the trend grows.

Retro.

We are a statistically-motivated
savage race. Among the worms,
we will rest. While we're alive,
we take it in stride—
We can't take it once we die.

Thespis the Tragedy

The reception, cold.
Dying up here, I used my
best delivery. The audience,
on their cell-phones too busy
to notice. Rather be six feet under
than face reality.

Not important, invisible
and unloved by my children,
Broken—They tried to put me
back together. The plastic
surgeons couldn't suture
me at the seams.

I eat my weight in my
shame. How can I compete?
Mass media and publicity
turned their backs on me,
I gave them performance,
God among insects.

Self-entitled, delusional
and self-important,
Self-destructive, the
show goes on with or
without the actor, with
or without the audience.

I cannot keep pretending
I am alive. *A number.*
Another statistic. Swooping
by, they pick my carcass
clean to the bone.
Vultures.

This Is The End

Lost and irrelevant,
Got to keep up. Always
trying to look
to the future by living
in the present and by looking
back at the past.

Gaze at the looking glass.
Does it blind your eyes?
Does it reveal skeletons
that you wish to hide?
If it blisters your skin,
it was not meant to be.

We're dropping like flies
and dead in the water.
Have you got the time
to attend a funeral for a friend?
Misguided by a force we
can't hope to control.

The end.

All you ever wanted
was to be somebody
in someone else's eyes.
Rendering of insignificance,
The opus is finished. Bow
your head and forget.

www.ingramcontent.com/pod-product-compliance
Lightning Source LLC
Chambersburg PA
CBHW021946040426
42448CB00008B/1264